IMAGES

of America

WALDAMEER PARK

Employees of the Erie Electric Motor Company stand ready to welcome visitors to Waldameer Park in this early-1900s photograph. Located just west of downtown overlooking Lake Erie, Waldameer Park provided a welcome escape on a hot summer day. (WP.)

ON THE COVER: A group of children enjoys Waldameer Park's fire engine ride. A popular attraction in the 1950s, the ride offered a tour of the park's grounds. (WP.)

IMAGES
of America

WALDAMEER PARK

Jim Futrell
Foreword by Paul Nelson

ARCADIA
PUBLISHING

Published by Arcadia Publishing
Charleston, South Carolina

Library of Congress Control Number: 2012947935

For all general information, please contact Arcadia Publishing:
Telephone 843-853-2070
Fax 843-853-0044
E-mail sales@arcadiapublishing.com
For customer service and orders:
Toll-Free 1-888-313-2665

Visit us on the Internet at www.arcadiapublishing.com

*To families . . . the one that supports my passion, the
one that has made Waldameer Park what it is, and
the thousands that have made memories there.*

CONTENTS

FOREWORD

Waldameer is for the community, and we are the caretakers of their park. We are the lucky people who have had the pleasure of running the "Good Ship called Waldameer."

Waldameer started out as a picnic grove that was purchased by the Erie Electric Motor Company and turned into a trolley car park that was named Waldameer, a German name for "Woods by the Sea." Back in the late 1800s, trolley companies purchased their electricity at a flat rate, and they needed places to go on weekends and holidays to entice people to use their trolleys to increase their weekend revenue. Thus, along came trolley parks across the country, but only a handful remain today.

Alex and Ruth Moeller, who were trusted with the responsibility to care for Waldameer, came to visit my parents in Dunkirk, New York, when I was 10 years old. I learned that they had an amusement park only 50 miles away and became very excited when invited to visit them the next summer. I could not wait for school to get out and have my parents take me to Erie, Pennsylvania, and boy, the weekend visit lasted until the school bells rang in September.

Alex Moeller took a great interest in an 11-year-old towheaded boy and before I left for home made a deal with me. . . . if I would come back every summer and live with and work for him until I finished my schooling and if I would take care of his wife (by then I called them Aunt Ruth and Uncle Alex), who was much younger than he, they would see that I, too, could take care of Waldameer for the people of Erie. I happily agreed, and we signed this with a warm handshake.

That was the beginning of a long, wonderful trip. By the age of 23, I had graduated from college, served my time in the Army, and came home to manage Waldameer.

I am 79 years old, and I am still in love with Waldameer and all the wonderful customers who make Waldameer what it is today.

—Paul Nelson

ACKNOWLEDGMENTS

No book can be possible without the support of numerous individuals and organizations. First and foremost, I would like to thank Paul Nelson of Waldameer Park. He has dedicated his life to making the park what it is and ensuring that it is successful for generations to come. His memories have been priceless in bringing this book to life as has the access he granted to the park archives. I would also like to thank Paul's family for all of their help—his wife, Lane Nelson; son-in-law and daughter, Steve and Nancy Gorman; and grandson and his wife, Brian and Allison Gorman.

Also providing critical support are two longtime Waldameer Park employees—Janet Little and Randy Skalos. They share a special affection for the park and have been very generous with their time and memorabilia. Good friend and fellow Arcadia author Dave Hahner also proved to be a valuable resource for images.

Four people deserve my special gratitude for making this book a reality—my wife and best friend, Marlowe, and our sons, Jimmy, Christopher, and Matthew. They share and appreciate my passion for amusement parks and understand when I had to spend time working on this book when they might have wanted me to do other things.

Finally, I would like to give a special thank-you to my parents, Jim and Joanne Futrell. When I was a young kid, just starting to discover my amusement park passion, they never dismissed my interest. They went out of their way to encourage and support it. They will always have a special place in my heart for that.

The images in this volume appear courtesy of Jim Futrell (JF), Dave Hahner (DH), Janet Little (JL), Randy Skalos (RS), and Waldameer Park (WP).

INTRODUCTION

For many Americans, summer just is not complete without a visit to an amusement park. In fact, each year America's approximately 400 amusement parks host nearly 300 million visitors.

One of the great things about amusement parks is the wide variety of facilities that people can visit. For many, amusement parks represent a vacation in and of itself at the huge theme park resorts in Orlando and California. Others see it as a daylong outing at a regional theme park with its record-breaking thrill rides. But the essence of the amusement park experience remains the classic, traditional-style amusement park with its shaded picnic grounds, action-packed midway, family-oriented rides, and nostalgic atmosphere.

That describes Waldameer Park. Since 1896, it has served as an escape for the people of northwestern Pennsylvania. Today, it represents a true survivor as one of just 11 of the hundreds of "trolley parks" that once dotted America that remains in operation.

While much of Waldameer's growth has come in the past three decades, it represents just part of a rich industry legacy that goes back over 500 years, when pleasure gardens spread throughout European cities from the 1500s to the early 1800s. They provided a place to escape the dreary conditions in teeming cities and featured many attractions that are familiar today, including landscaped gardens, live entertainment, fireworks, dancing, games, and even predecessors to today's merry-go-round, roller coaster, and Ferris wheel rides.

In the late 1700s, America was emerging into a nation of its own, and as the country grew, simplified versions of the European pleasure garden started to appear. One example was Vauxhall Gardens, named after a renowned pleasure garden in London, which opened in New York City around 1767 and featured one of America's first carousels.

The industry really flourished in the decades following the Civil War. With the Industrial Revolution sweeping across the nation, people flocked from the countryside into the cities, creating conditions similar to what existed in Europe a few centuries earlier. Those cities were linked by America's burgeoning transportation infrastructure, which spread throughout the country. As it was making the nation smaller, it was also playing a critical role in developing the amusement park industry, as people with increasing amounts of money and free time sought to escape.

Among the first developers of amusement parks were railroads, which sought to build passenger traffic by developing several amusement parks, usually in the rural outskirts of cities. Steamship companies also pioneered the concept establishing resorts along waterfronts in the Northeast and the Midwest. But it was really the spread of the trolley that truly established the amusement park as an American icon.

In the wake of the opening of the first electric-powered street rail line in Richmond, Virginia, in 1888, hundreds of trolley lines popped up around the country almost overnight. To maximize revenue, the operators sought a way to attract riders during lightly used evenings and weekend periods. Opening amusement resorts provided the ideal solution. Typically built at the end of the trolley lines, these resorts initially were simple operations consisting of picnic facilities, dance halls, restaurants, games, and a few amusement rides. But as simple as they were, they tapped a huge unmet demand and soon spread across America. Waldameer Park was one of those places, opening on the site of a popular picnic grove.

But like most trolley parks, it was not always an easy ride for Waldameer Park. Around World War I, trolley companies began to tire of being in the amusement park business. Many closed, while others were sold to private operators. Waldameer fell into the hands of a local bank who leased it to several operators, including Alex Moeller, a German sailor who came to America to seek his fortune.

Following the prosperity of the 1920s, the hardship of the Depression further eroded the number of amusement parks. But under the guidance of Moeller, Waldameer survived and managed to thrive during World War II when materials shortages and travel restrictions put many of its peers out of business.

America emerged from World War II as a changed nation. While a strong economy and a population looking to put the war behind it provided a much-needed boost to the industry, returning veterans were focused on pursuing the American dream. They were leaving the urban centers where most amusement parks were located and flocked to the suburbs to raise their new families. Attractions like kiddie lands and theme parks provided additional competition to older parks that were struggling with aging infrastructure, declining neighborhoods, and ownership issues.

Spurred by the opening of Disneyland in 1955, attention in the amusement industry soon shifted to large corporate theme parks that quickly spread throughout the United States. While many older parks were left behind, others managed to change and adapt.

Fortunately, Waldameer fell in the latter category. It continued to add attractions in the 1950s and in the 1960s launched a major modernization program led by Paul Nelson. Nelson's parents were friends with the Moellers, and once he visited the park at age 11, he began a lifelong love affair with the park that culminated in him assuming full ownership in 1978.

It was a time when many other family-owned amusement parks were closing in the face of rising property values, aging facilities, and the loss of the industrial base that provided much of their critical picnic business. But after working his whole life to gain control of Waldameer Park, Nelson was not about to join that club. Starting in 1985, he spent over $30 million on an ongoing transformation that continues to this day. What was once a quiet local escape is now a major regional attraction that has outlasted several larger corporate-owned competitors.

Even today, with advances in technology, demands of time, and changes in consumer tastes, the appeal of amusement parks remains unchanged. Having a relaxed summer day with family and friends, pushing the limits on the rides, indulging in foods one would not consider consuming elsewhere, and making memories to last a lifetime combine to create an experience that cannot be duplicated.

Waldameer Park represents a rare breed in today's amusement industry, a family-owned and -operated amusement park that through shrewd management and wise investment has been able to survive and thrive in a changing world. Enjoy the story of Waldameer Park.

In the early years of Waldameer Park, an important part of the experience was to enjoy the breeze riding an open-air trolley car to and from the park. These cars were for summer use only and were stored at the park during the winter. (WP.)

One

WOODS BY THE SEA
1896–1919

In the late 1800s, Erie, Pennsylvania, was typical of so many places in America. As the nation was emerging as an industrial powerhouse, people were flocking to the city to work in new industries. With crowded conditions and newfound affluence, people sought ways to escape and be entertained. One way to escape was to visit Waldameer Park.

Founded by the Erie Electric Motor Company, which itself began operations in 1889, it was one of the hundreds of trolley parks opening throughout the country during that period. The trolley company purchased a 65-acre parcel overlooking Lake Erie, four miles west of downtown. Then known as Hoffman's Grove, the land was already a popular picnic destination. In a 1909 history of Erie County, author John Miller describes the grove as having, "No finer specimens of the chestnut, red or black oak, cucumber magnolia or hemlock spruce are to be found anywhere." This flora, combined with the lakefront location and German heritage of the city made it easy for the trolley company to choose a name for the new business—Waldameer—German for "woods by the sea."

In those early years, Waldameer Park was like most trolley parks of the era. Picnicking, dancing, and live entertainment were the main attractions. With the neighboring Presque Isle State Park still a swamp, Waldameer Park was also considered the main beach in Erie, and patrons flocked there to enjoy the cooling lake waters on a hot summer day. The park was almost entirely self-sufficient. A gas well was dug on property to provide backup electrical power, and water from a spring was stored in a 20,000-gallon reservoir for use in the park.

By 1902, Waldameer was a well-established operation, and a park brochure described the facility as: "One of the pleasantest of pleasure's hunting grounds. Nowhere can one find a prettier or more healthful retreat. Its combination of lake and beach, and wild groves produce a variety of land and water scenes that are most charming." By then its first ride, a carousel, had already appeared.

It would take approximately 30 minutes to make the four-mile journey from downtown Erie to Waldameer Park. This 1908 picture shows a trolley car arriving at the park and heading to the car station. (JF.)

Car Station at Waldemere Park, Erie, Pa.

The car station was an important feature of early trolley parks. Waldameer was no different, with riders disembarking, waiting for, and boarding trolleys near the current location of the Dodgems. (JF.)

From the car station, it was a quick walk to Waldameer Park's main entrance, near the current location of today's Music Express. Then as now, the carousel was one of the first attractions riders experienced. (JF.)

This photograph of Waldameer Park's original main gate shows the park closed for the season. It gives a great view of the detail of the front ticket booth. The entrance arch was a park fixture for years. (WP.)

One of the first things visitors would encounter was the carousel. Waldameer Park's original carousel opened in 1901. In 1905, the building seen in the picture above was built for $7,500 to house a new carousel from T.M. Harton of Pittsburgh. The carousel building remains today as home to Waldameer's current merry-go-round. (WP.)

As it is today, the Main Promenade is the heart of Waldameer Park. This picture from 1909 shows a crowded day on the midway with visitors flocking to the carousel on the right and game buildings on the left. While most of the buildings have been replaced and there are more attractions today, probably the most dramatic difference visible in this photograph is the way the park's visitors dressed in this era. (JF.)

14

Everybody here but you — Waldameer Park, Erie, Pa.

As the caption on this postcard says, Waldameer Park was a popular destination in the early 20th century. This view of the midway is looking north toward Lake Erie, which is concealed by the thick trees. The round shape on top of the building in the center is a large penny to promote the penny arcade contained within. (JF.)

Waldameer Park, Erie, Pa.

Looking back down the midway toward the entrance shows crowds gathered in the carousel building on the left. The large structure across the midway, topped by flags, is the entrance to the Figure Eight roller coaster. (WP.)

Penny arcades have been part of the amusement park experience for more than 100 years, and one has been a part of Waldameer Park since the turn of the 20th century. Of course in those days, it did live up to its name with all games costing a penny. Among the most popular were mutoscopes, which flipped a series of cards resulting in a short movie. (WP.)

Another popular early feature at Waldameer Park was the bowling alley. With five lanes, this bowling alley actually resembled the skeeball alleys popular at today's amusement parks and arcades, rather than the more common 10-pin bowling. (JF.)

Picnicking was one of the most popular diversions at early amusement parks. Waldameer Park had a 10-acre area set aside for picnickers. Customers would usually bring their baskets out on the trolley and leave them at a table for the day. It is a tradition that continues at the park today. (JF.)

For those visitors who did not bring a picnic basket or wanted to make the day a more special occasion, the park offered a café located in the woods. (JL.)

Another popular attraction at early amusement parks was dancing. It provided the perfect opportunity for couples to get close during much more conservative times. In 1902, Waldameer Park built its first dance hall. Holding up to 150 couples, it offered dancing every evening except on Mondays and Saturdays. (JF.)

The bands in the dance hall were not the only form of entertainment. In the early 20th century, live entertainment, including bands and summer stock theater, was one of the biggest draws for amusement parks. Waldameer included a large band shell in the early years, offering a full variety of entertainment. (JF.)

18

One of the earliest rides at Waldameer Park was the Razzle Dazzle or Whirly-Gig. This simple attraction was human powered and was patented in 1891 by William Mangels of Coney Island in New York. It was a common attraction at amusement parks in the early 20th century. (JF.)

Another popular early ride was the Aerial Swing. A simple attraction, it offered patrons the chance to soar amongst the trees in cars that rotated around a central tower from which they were suspended. This ride was one of Waldameer's longest-lived rides, changing cars on several occasions to keep up with the times. (JF.)

Figure Eight, Waldameer Park, Erie, Pa.

Roller coasters have been part of Waldameer Park since 1902 when T.M. Harton built the Figure Eight. Later known as the Dip the Dips, it was a gentle ride in which cars traveled along a figure eight–shaped layout. Hundreds of these types of rides were constructed around the country with Harton building dozens throughout the region. As was common in the era, Harton operated rides on a concession basis, owning and operating it and paying rent to the trolley company. Harton of Pittsburgh, Pennsylvania, was an important figure in the early development of the park. In addition to assembling the carousel in 1905, he built its first fun house, the House of Hilarity, in 1907. Another roller coaster, the Scenic Railway, operated from 1907 to 1919. Fred Ingersoll, also of Pittsburgh, built it, and unfortunately, no pictures are known to exist. (Both, JF.)

While Waldameer Park's rides and attractions were a popular draw, its wooded grounds were as much a diversion in those early days. This picture shows couples promenading alongside the café. (WP.)

Scene at Waldameer Park, Erie, Pa.

The heavy shade provided a cooling summer respite for couples to escape. Peaceful paths wound through the grounds cutting through the thick tree cover. (WP.)

In addition to the main portion of the park, the beach, located 70 feet below the midway along the shores of Lake Erie, was a major center of activity. Getting to the beach required a hike through a ravine. (JF.)

The ravine hike ended at a 1,000-foot-long boardwalk, constructed in 1901, which crossed a lagoon and led to the beach. (JF.)

Most early amusement parks included at least a modest body of water as boating was a popular diversion. Waldameer Park featured this large lagoon just behind the beach. (JF.)

This picture shows several couples enjoying rowboats in the lagoon with the boardwalk cutting across it to the bathhouse at the beach. (JF.)

This picture from 1919 shows the boardwalk leading back to the ravine pathway from the beach. Several rowboats are visible, waiting for customers to use them. Canoes were also available. (WP.)

Another view of the boardwalk shows it much higher than previous views indicating that it might have been rebuilt at a higher level to allow boats to pass underneath. (JF.)

Waldameer Park was not just for day visits. Many people would set up camp for all or part of the summer to take advantage of the cooler weather along the lakefront. This 1910 picture shows Camp Clemons at the park. (WP.)

For many people, swimming was not part of a visit to the beach. But that did not mean they would not enjoy the water. It was the perfect place to relax, cool off, and watch the waves roll up on shore. (JF.)

For those that chose to take the plunge, Waldameer Park offered a 110-foot-long bathhouse, which offered 160 individual dressing rooms. Joseph Frank, a prominent Erie architect, designed it. It was common practice during that era to offer bathing suits for rental. (JF.)

This picture from 1909 shows a number of individual dressing stalls lined up along the beach. It also shows one of the piers that was built into the lake to permit swimming, fishing, or strolling. An observation tower can be seen on the right. (JF.)

Picture postcards of individuals enjoying Waldameer Park's beach were a popular souvenir in the early 20th century, and a full line was produced. They profiled typical activities on the beach like searching for treasures in the sand, walking the dog, or seeing what the surf washed in. (Above, JF; below, JL.)

Waldameer Beach, Erie, Pa. 571.

Other cards, such as the one above dated 1907, showed a couple gazing out across the waters while their dog runs through the surf. The one below highlighted people hanging out on the beach in what is definitely not beachwear. (Above, JF; below, JL.)

Bathing Beach at Waldameer Park, Erie, Pa.

Two

HIGHS AND LOWS
1920s–1930s

Like the industry as a whole, the personality of Waldameer Park changed in the years following World War I with rides becoming more common and more popular. It was a time that the park grew up with several major rides making their debuts. George Sinclair, who owned Meyer's Lake Park in Canton, Ohio, built many of the rides. Sinclair was a major concessionaire at Waldameer, building not only the Ravine Flyer roller coaster but also the Mill Chute, a boat ride with a splashdown finale. The beach remained popular and was linked to the rest of the park by a funicular called the Toonerville Trolley.

Like most trolley companies, what was now the Buffalo & Lake Erie Traction Company was looking to exit the amusement park business and turned control of Waldameer over to Marine Bank. Among the parties the bank leased the park to was Alex Moeller. A former German sailor, Moeller migrated to Erie in 1913, stopping first in New York where he sold hot dogs at Coney Island. He worked in hotel food service and started selling hot dogs at Waldameer, later becoming general manager of the park and eventually coming to own the facility.

Hundreds of amusement parks closed throughout the country during the Depression, and those that remained struggled to survive. Waldameer also met its share of unique challenges. In addition to the tough economic times, a Chestnut blight killed off many of the majestic trees that gave the park its name. Its beach was losing traffic to the new Presque Isle State Park, trolley service was ended in 1935, the Dip the Dips and Ravine Flyer roller coasters were removed in 1937 and 1938, respectively, and the dance hall burned down in 1937. But Waldameer was able to survive and continue to bring in the crowds by offering low-cost attractions, such as free talking movies, providing a welcome respite from the tough times.

As Waldameer Park moved into the 1920s and 1930s, the entrance arch continued to welcome visitors. The original Figure Eight still greeted visitors but had long since been transformed into the Dip the Dips. (JF.)

This view of the midway from October 1924 shows the Dip the Dips when it was known as the Coney Island Scenic Coaster. The park has been put to bed for the season, and boarded-up buildings and barren trees are a scene few visitors experienced. (WP.)

Looking south from the north end of Waldameer Park in 1937, the carousel building is visible on the left. The arched building on the right is a refreshment stand featuring frozen custard. Today, it remains the location of Waldameer's main refreshment stand. (WP.)

Following a visit to Elitch Gardens in Denver, Colorado, in the late 1920s, Alex Moeller decided to replicate its domed carousel building south of the existing carousel to spread out the park. The old carousel building was converted into a dodgem structure featuring the popular bumper car ride. For several years, a Whip ride operated between the two carousel buildings. (JF.)

Located farther away from the main park activities, ridership dropped on the carousel, and the ride was soon returned to its original location. The home of Waldameer's carousel has not changed since then. (WP.)

In November 1924, Waldameer Park's original dance hall was destroyed in a fire. Given the importance of dancing to the park, there was no doubt that it would be replaced. By the following April, construction was well under way on the replacement structure. (Both, WP.)

Rainbow Gardens was the new ballroom, so named in a contest due to its multicolored floor tiles. (WP.)

The inside of Rainbow Gardens was an expansive structure easily capable of holding the throngs flocking to the park to enjoy the sounds of increasing popular big bands that were touring the country. (JL.)

The Hofbrau German Beer Garden originally opened in 1909. Incorporating the original band shell and seating 2,000 people, it was known for its singing waiters. When Prohibition was enacted in 1919, the restaurant had to stop serving beer, but it resumed in 1932 with its repeal. To avoid using the word beer in those sensitive post-Prohibition times, the restaurant was called the German Village. But to ensure that visitors knew that beer was available, Waldameer distributed tickets good for one free glass. (Both, WP.)

During the Depression, Waldameer, like most amusement parks, offered free attractions to bring in people in cash-constrained times. One of the most popular was Monkey Island, which featured several monkeys living in their own world. (WP.)

This early morning view of the midway shows the entrance to the Mill Chute ride, one of the attractions erected in the 1920s by George Sinclair. (WP.)

The Mill Chute was a popular ride in the 1920s, the forerunner of today's log flumes. Boats would float through a trough and be hauled up a chain, similar to that of a roller coaster, to plunge down into a pool. It was much dryer than today's water rides but a cooling diversion on a hot summer day nonetheless. (Both, WP.)

As times changed and flying became a fascination with the public, Waldameer's Aerial Swing, like those at most amusement parks, was switched from the Victorian-era wicker gondolas to those that resembled airplanes. This gave an aging ride a much-needed shot in the arm as people flocked to it to soar in an airplane. (Both, WP.)

The 1920s were known as the first Golden Age of roller coasters, and parks sought to take advantage of technology to build faster and steeper rides. In 1922, concessionaire George Sinclair built the Ravine Flyer. Designed by John Miller, history's greatest roller coaster designer, it took advantage of the park's hilly terrain and crossed over Peninsula Drive twice during its run. This is the only known picture of the ride. (WP.)

A fatal accident on the Ravine Flyer in 1938 so upset Alex Moeller's wife, L. Ruth, that he immediately removed the ride. While it was demolished, the Ravine Flyer's station was converted a picnic pavilion, a role it continues to play to this day. (WP.)

Miniature trains have been a favorite attraction at amusement parks since the early 20th century. Waldameer Park's first known miniature train was manufactured by the Dayton Fun House Company of Dayton, Ohio, and installed in 1924. (WP.)

The open-air train provided a tour of the park, including a trip past the Mill Chute, which can be seen in the background. (WP.)

This view of the midway from the late 1930s shows a wide-open expanse much different than the action-packed midway of today. (WP.)

Today, sweepers roaming the midways of amusement parks are a common sight. This photograph from the 1930s shows some Waldameer employees clowning around on the midway with their brooms. (WP.)

With the public seeking new ways to be thrilled, numerous new rides were invented in the 1920s, including the Caterpillar. Riders were seated in cars that traveled over an undulating track, much like today's Himalaya and Music Express rides. A canopy then covered the cars, giving couples the chance to sneak a kiss. This model was likely built by Traver Engineering of Beaver Falls, Pennsylvania. (WP.)

Another popular ride invented in the 1920s was the Custer Cars. Invented in the mid-1920s, the ride was manufactured by the Custer Specialty Company of Dayton, Ohio. With automobiles just coming into the American mainstream, the battery-powered cars were quite popular with the younger set and predated the turnpike and go-kart rides found in today's amusement parks. (WP.)

The public's increased thirst for thrills following World War I did not just bring new rides to the park, but also changed Waldameer's existing rides. The Figure Eight, Waldameer's original roller coaster, was revitalized, replacing its mild dips with deeper drops, as seen in this winter photograph. (WP.)

This picture of the Dip the Dips was taken in its final season of 1937. By now, the aging ride was losing riders and was in need of increased maintenance during the hard times of the Depression. It was demolished at the end of the season. (WP.)

This picture shows an action-packed day on the northern part of Waldameer's midway, near the shore of Lake Erie. Just to the left of the Caterpillar is Bluebeard's Castle, a large fun house. (WP.)

This picture shows Bluebeard's Castle on a quieter day in 1936. These types of fun houses were quite popular in the 1920s and were found at amusement parks throughout the country. (WP.)

By the 1920s, the hike through the ravine and across the lagoon on the boardwalk to the beach had been replaced by the Toonerville Trolley. This funicular connected the main part of the park to the beach, saving patrons a long, hot hike on a summer day. (WP.)

The beach was still a popular draw, as seen in this postcard dated 1924. A waterslide into Lake Erie was a main feature. (JF.)

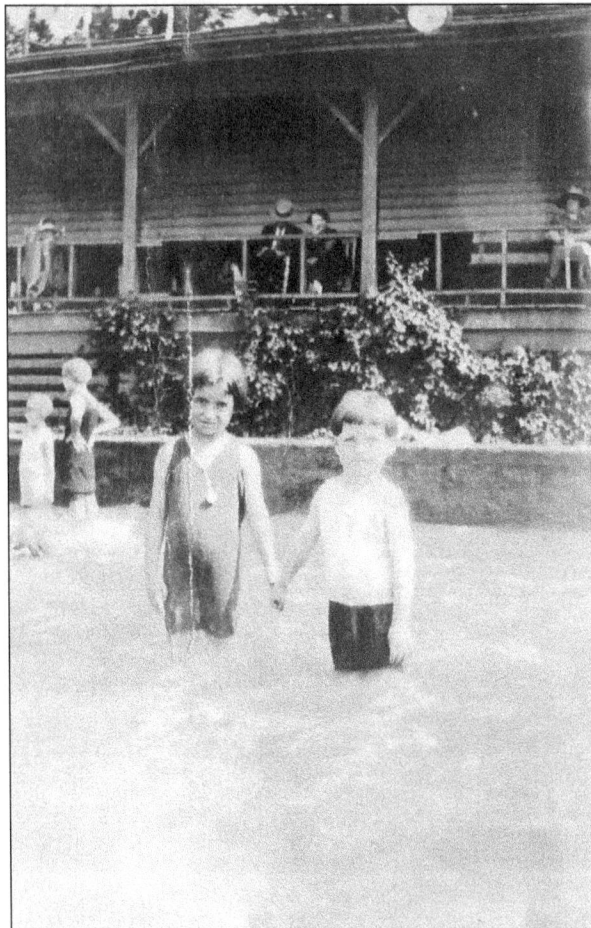

Another new attraction at the beach in the 1920s was the swimming pool. Seen at the bottom of the picture above, it provides an option to the waves of Lake Erie. Swimming pools became a popular attraction at amusement parks in the 1920s, and many amusement parks that opened during this era were built around large pools. The two children at left are enjoying the shallow end of the pool in 1927. (Above, JF; left, WP.)

By the late 1920s, the beach at Waldameer Park was dotted by cottages that were a little more substantial than their predecessors two decades earlier. It was still a popular destination for people to spend part of their summer. (JF.)

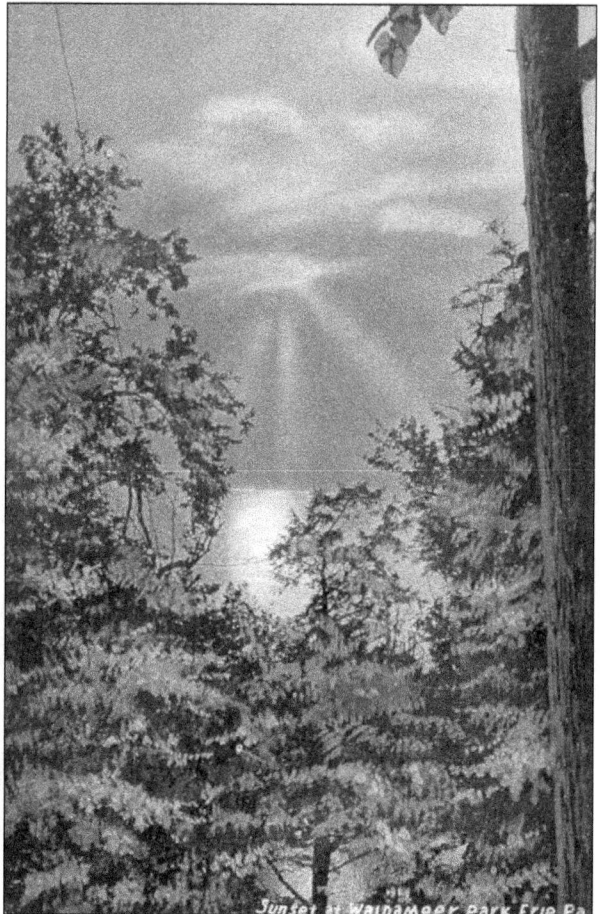

Since its earliest days, one of the greatest charms of a visit to Waldameer Park was to see the sunset over Lake Erie. From the upper portion of the park, the sunset poked through the trees, signifying another evening at the park, where dancing in the ballroom set the pace. (JL.)

47

During the early 20th century, Waldameer Park was much more than an amusement park, but with its beach and summer cottages, it was a neighborhood in and of itself. This lead to independent businesses setting up shop. One was the Cooper grocery, shown above, which also included the family's residence and a confectionery. In addition to the store, the Cooper family also operated the games in the park. Another business was Wettekins grocery store and ice cream parlor (below). (Both, JF.)

Throughout the 1920s and 1930s, Alex Moeller (second row, fourth from the left), shown with park superintendent Harvey Pettis next to him, took on greater responsibility for operating the park. Starting as a hot dog vendor, he ended up leasing the park and taking over all of the rides before assuming complete ownership. (WP.)

By the end of the 1930s, Waldameer Park had a completely different personality. The sedate diversion of strolls through the woods had given way to high-speed thrill rides as the main attraction. But the greatest change was the elimination of the trolley line that gave birth to the park. Seen here is the new entrance gate that welcomed the new preferred means of getting to the park—the automobile. (WP.)

This aerial view of Waldameer Park likely dates the late 1930s. In 1937, a fire destroyed the Rainbow Gardens Ballroom. Since funding did not exist to rebuild the structure, Waldameer constructed an outdoor dance floor for the 1938 season. However, due to the unpredictable nature of the weather, the new concept met with limited success. The outdoor dance hall can be seen in the upper left. Also visible in this rare view are the two carousel buildings, the original from 1905 and the 1920s version (bottom center), which, by this point, was likely used as a picnic pavilion. Changing times are evident as all signs of the trolley tracks are gone, while parking lots dominate to the left and right. (WP.)

Three

THE JOY SPOT OF ERIE
1940s–1970s

As the darkness of the Depression began to fade, the clouds of war reared their head. It was a challenging time for the amusement park industry as travel restrictions, fuel rationing, and material shortages closed many parks, while the booming wartime economy provided a much-needed financial boost to others.

Although attendance initially fell at Waldameer, when the ban on pleasure driving was lifted in 1944, the park saw a 50-percent increase in business. In 1945, as the war was winding down, two events cemented the future of Waldameer. After leasing the facility for two decades, Alex Moeller finally was able to purchase the park. That same year, a family friend, the Nelsons, arrived with their 11-year-old son Paul. He was enamored with the park and soon began working there. It began a relationship that continues to this day.

A series of storms in the 1930s and 1940s wiped out the remainder of the beach. However, with the war ending, Waldameer again looked to the future. After five years of planning, a roller coaster returned to the park in 1951 in the form of the Comet. In response to the postwar baby boom, more kiddie rides were added in a separate kiddie land.

The growing park enjoyed a better fate in those postwar years than many of its counterparts who were hard pressed to remain relevant in a changing world. Throughout the 1950s and 1960s, amusement parks faced urban decay, aging facilities, and the rise of interstates and air travel that brought once distant destinations closer.

As many of Waldameer's larger counterparts closed, Nelson was taking on a higher profile, having assumed the role of general manager in 1957 and full management control upon Moeller's death in 1965. He began modernizing the aging facility, replacing the wooden concession stands with all-steel buildings, filling ravines to increase useable acreage by one-third, upgrading utilities, and planting new trees. Throughout the 1970s, improvements continued, and many rides and attractions that remain popular to this day, including the Whacky Shack, Pirate's Cove, and L. Ruth Express, made their debuts.

Waldameer Park began the 1940s on a high note with the replacement of Rainbow Gardens with an all-new version. Following the failed experiment with outdoor dancing, patrons flocked back to the new indoor ballroom that had a capacity of 3,000. It remains in use to this day. (JF.)

In October 1941, one of the park's oldest features, the German Village restaurant, was destroyed by fire. A dinner for 1,500 was under way at the time, and while everyone was safely evacuated, 11 people were injured, and a waitress perished when she went back inside to retrieve her coat. (WP.)

By 1942, America was fully involved in World War II. With materials in short supply, the park was sometimes forced to improvise. For instance, in 1942, they paved the parking lot with scrap rubber. But despite the restrictions, the economy of Erie was booming as factories were operating at capacity to support the war effort. As a result, Waldameer's midways were crowded with those that could make it to the park. (WP.)

Waldameer Park fully supported the war effort, holding benefit days for the Army-Navy relief fund. In addition, several rides were given patriotic names and paint jobs, including the train, which was renamed the Victory Special. (WP.)

A summer afternoon at Waldameer finds the park crowded with families. In the background, a crowd gathers around the Monkey Island, while a photographer takes pictures of a child nearby. (WP.)

WALDAMEER BEACH, SHOWING COTTAGES AND HOTEL ERIE. PA

During the 1930s and 1940s, a number of storms washed away the remainder of Waldameer's beach. To stop the continuing erosion, the US Army Corps of Engineers built a large break wall out of large stones parallel to the shoreline. Waldameer's beach has not been used since then. (JF.)

Through the 1940s, the north end of Waldameer Park was anchored by a large concession stand and the Fun in the Dark. The Fun in the Dark was built by Pretzel Amusement Company of New Jersey. Founded by William Cassidy, who is credited with inventing the tracked dark ride, Pretzel built over 1,400 throughout its existence. (WP.)

Replacing the fun house, Fun in the Dark was a classic dark ride in which patrons rode two-person cars along a winding track through darkened rooms where a variety of mechanical stunts would surprise riders. Included along its 425 feet of track were 10 animated figures, including Laughing Sam. It was sold following the 1950 season. (RS.)

One of the first true thrill rides to adorn amusement park midways was the Loop-O-Plane. Invented in 1933 by Lee Eyerly, founder of Eyerly Aircraft Company of Salem, Oregon, it flipped four people completely upside down. Later versions featured two cars. (WP.)

In this picture, Waldameer's Loop-O-Plane operators take a few minutes to relax. The Loop-O-Plane was located in the heart of the midway in front of the Aerial Swing. (WP.)

By the 1940s, the carousel has been relocated back to its original building. By this time, kiddie rides, which started appearing at amusement parks in the 1920s, were well established at Waldameer Park. One of the first was the Blue Goose, located next to the carousel, which gave children rides in oversized geese and storks. (WP.)

Another classic amusement park attraction that has entertained Waldameer Park patrons for decades was the bumper cars. Bumper cars were invented in the years following World War I and soon were found in most amusement parks. While the cars and buildings have changed at Waldameer, the thrills remain the same. (WP.)

To help offset the drop in traffic during World War II, Waldameer Park would offer free acts on its stage. Located in the northeastern corner of the park, the stage was a longtime fixture. (WP.)

The stage was a center of activity for the community and offered everything from live entertainment to ethnic festivals to political rallies. (WP.)

This picture looks toward the northwestern section of Waldameer Park in the 1940s. The picnic shelter in the background is the former station of the Ravine Flyer. On the left is the refreshment stand, which dates back to the earliest days of the park. (WP.)

Several rides made their first appearance in the 1940s, including the Flying Scooter. The Flying Scooter was invented in the late 1930s and immediately became a popular attraction. In this picture, several patrons are enjoying a band concert, while the cars fly by. (JF.)

Built by the Bisch Rocco Company of Chicago, Illinois, the Flying Scooter was one of the first participatory rides. Riders would be able to control the motion of each tub by moving a large wing mounted in the front back and forth. Even today, the ride remains popular and "snapping" the cables is considered the ultimate accomplishment for aficionados of the Flying Scooter. (Above, JF; right, WP.)

In 1944, with wartime restrictions easing, Waldameer Park was able to undertake an expansion and add three rides, including the Whip. The ride features two-person cars that "whip" around the corners increasing the sensation of speed. (WP.)

By 1944, the Whip was a longtime favorite at amusement parks. It was originally invented in 1918 by William F. Mangels of Coney Island, New York. It is considered one of the first "flat" rides to operate at amusement parks, the forerunner of today's spinning rides. Waldameer's Whip was sold following the 1947 season. (WP.)

The park also added a Ferris wheel to its lineup in 1944. Originally invented in 1893 by George Ferris for the World's Columbian Exposition, Waldameer's wheel was manufactured by the Eli Bridge Company of Illinois. Eli Bridge created a smaller version of the Ferris wheel in 1900 that was perfect for carnivals and amusement parks and continues to be an industry staple. (WP.)

The Whip, Flying Scooter, and Ferris wheel comprised a ride area that anchored the northwestern portion of the park between the main midway and Rainbow Gardens. (WP.)

The third ride added to Waldameer Park in 1944 was the Tumble Bug. Manufactured by Traver Engineering of Beaver Falls, Pennsylvania, the ride was invented in the mid-1920s and consisted of six circular cars that travel along an undulating circular track, 100 feet in diameter. It operated until the late 1950s. (WP.)

As Waldameer Park was adding modern rides in the 1940s, it was also updating some of its originals. In 1946, the Aerial Swing ride was modernized with stainless-steel Buck Rogers–style rocket ships replacing the airplane-shaped cars. (WP.)

Waldameer Park added a new train ride in 1947, purchasing it from the National Amusement Devices Company (NAD) of Dayton, Ohio. NAD was one of the largest manufacturers of amusement rides in the mid-20th century. The ride was originally located next to the carousel. (WP.)

In 1948, upgrades continued at Waldameer Park with the Caterpillar replacing the Whip next to Rainbow Gardens. Built by the Allan Herschell Company of North Tonawanda, New York, another major manufacturer in the mid-20th century, it was an updated version of the Caterpillar that operated at the park in the 1920s. (WP.)

This picture shows a busy day on the midway in the late 1940s. The new National Amusement Devices train ride is picking up a load of riders on the left, while two of the park's original kiddie rides—the Blue Goose, next to the carousel, and the airplane swing to its right—are popular with the younger set. (WP.)

Waldameer Park's Mill Chute ride underwent a transformation in the years following World War II. The large splashdown hill was removed and replaced with a much smaller drop, and the ride was renamed Mill Run. Initially, the trough through which boats floated was covered with a tunnel, but that was soon removed. (WP.)

When the tunnel was removed from the Mill Run, the expansive grassy area in the middle of the ride was turned into a miniature golf course called Tricky Golf. Miniature golf was a popular diversion in the 1950s and 1960s with courses springing up around the country. Many amusement parks also added them, but Waldameer's was gone by the late 1970s. Not only did golfers have to contend with obstacles on the course, but they were also challenged by a water hazard of a different type—the Mill Run trough. (Above, WP; below, JF.)

In 1946, Waldameer Park announced plans to build a new roller coaster. It took four years until conditions were right to begin construction The Caterpillar and Fun in the Dark rides were sold to accommodate the expansion, and a site was selected next to the carousel where the train operated. The train was relocated. (WP.)

This picture shows park employees celebrating the arrival of another load of lumber for the Comet. A young Paul Nelson (fourth from the left), who was still in high school, skipped football practice to assist with the delivery. When this picture appeared in the local newspaper, his coach caught him and made him run laps the entire next practice. (WP.)

To design and build the Comet, Waldameer Park hired the Philadelphia Toboggan Company (PTC) of Germantown, Pennsylvania, the leading roller coaster manufacturer of the era. PTC's lead designer created a family ride, standing 37 feet tall with a first drop of 25 feet. Still a popular attraction, the ride reaches a maximum speed of 25 miles per hour. (Both, JF.)

Despite the opening of new rides following World War II, traditional attractions such as the park's 1905 carousel still remained popular. It is shown here in 1951. (WP.)

Amusement parks started opening separate kiddie lands at their facilities in the late 1920s. But with the postwar baby boom in full force in the 1950s, they became commonplace. After having only a few kiddie rides, Waldameer Park greatly expanded its selection in the 1950s, consolidating them in their own special area. (JF.)

Among the leading manufacturers of kiddie rides during this era was the Allan Herschell Company of North Tonawanda, New York. It produced a full line and could outfit a complete kiddie land. One of its products was the Sky Fighter, featuring miniature rocket ships. Waldameer's Sky Fighter remains a popular kiddie attraction. (WP.)

Another major manufacturer of kiddie rides was Ben Schiff and Associates of Miami Beach, Florida. The company provided Waldameer's kiddie boat and pony cart rides, both of which are still entertaining Waldameer's youngest guests. (JF.)

71

Monkey Island remained a popular attraction well into the 1950s. Spectators still enjoyed spending time watching the Rhesus monkeys frolic in their own special habitat, but by the middle of the decade, the park was forced to close the longtime attraction. Reportedly, America's fledgling space program used so many monkeys that the park could not replenish its supply. (Both, WP.)

While Monkey Island ceased to operate, Waldameer Park moved on. This postcard of Monkey Island shows two popular rides in the background. Behind the Flying Scooter is the Looper. Another creation of the Allan Herschell Company, it featured circular cars in which riders could flip themselves upside down. The Looper was located at the current site of the Tilt-A-Whirl. (WP.)

Alex Moeller's wife, L. Ruth, loved gardening and for many years maintained a rock garden in front of the park office. (JF.)

The park's Skyview Ferris wheel met an untimely end in the late 1950s. By now, Paul Nelson had worked his way up to general manager. Moeller asked him to move the Skyview from the south end of the park to the current location of the gift shop. Rather than disassembling it, Nelson had a crane lift the entire ride and transport it down the midway. According to Nelson, the crane hit a bump, and both it and the wheel tipped over. The Ferris wheel was a total loss. The next morning Moeller asked Nelson if the job was complete. "It's done," Nelson replied. While Moeller was not happy, he chalked it up as a learning experience for Nelson, as long as he did not do something like that again. Waldameer Park would be without a Ferris wheel until the 1990s. (JF.)

As Waldameer Park entered the 1960s, more contemporary rides were installed. The Flying Coaster was placed next to the former location of Monkey Island in 1962. Manufactured by Aeroaffiliates of Fort Worth, Texas, the ride featured eight cars that travel along a circular track. Each car would travel over a ramp and go airborne, before being hydraulically lowered to the ground. It operated until 1994. (JF.)

Around 1964, the Tilt-A-Whirl was added next to Rainbow Gardens where the Whip, Caterpillar, and Looper previously operated. Built by Sellner Manufacturing of Faribault, Minnesota, it has been a midway staple since its invention in 1928 with seven cars spinning around an undulating platform. It remains in operation. (DH.)

Also joining the ride lineup in 1964 was the Scrambler. First manufactured in 1955 by the Eli Bridge Company of Jacksonville, Illinois, the Scrambler was installed on the south end of Waldameer's midway, where it remains to this day. (WP.)

By the early 1970s, Waldameer Park was evolving. Midway staples, such as the carousel and Comet, remained popular. Meanwhile in the background is the Scrambler. And although, the Aerial Swing with its rocket ship cars still spun, its days were numbered. (WP.)

In 1970, Waldameer undertook one of its largest postwar projects, the Whacky Shack. The park had been without a dark ride since Fun in the Dark was sold in 1950. After being impressed with some of his work at other amusement parks, Bill Tracy, the leading dark ride designer of the era, was contracted by the park to construct the ride. (RS.)

The ride was erected on the north end of the midway in a building measuring 50 by 82 feet. Behind its soaring colorful facade, the ride features 488 feet of track over two levels. Of the 46 dark rides built by Tracy, Whacky Shack is one of six still in operation. (JL.)

The Whacky Shack is the epitome of a classic amusement park dark ride. It has 18 stunts, ranging from the traditional monsters and skeletons to a swooping drop, revolving barrel, loud noises, and lighting effects. (Both, DH.)

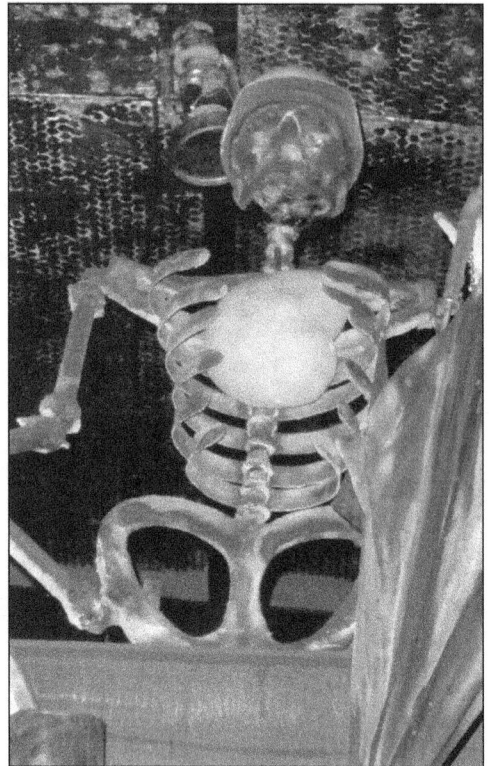

Whacky Shack was a huge success, and two years later, Bill Tracy was again hired by Waldameer Park to design a new attraction. Pirate's Cove is an updated version of a traditional fun house. Known as a walk-through attraction, customers make their way through a series rooms with a variety of stunts. (JL.)

Over 15 stunts are featured in Pirate's Cove, including the shuffleboard, the cyclone room, a tilt room, the barrel maze, the jail maze, and the swinging bridge. Pirate's Cove was one of 15 walk-through attractions designed by Bill Tracy and is one of only two remaining in operation. (DH.)

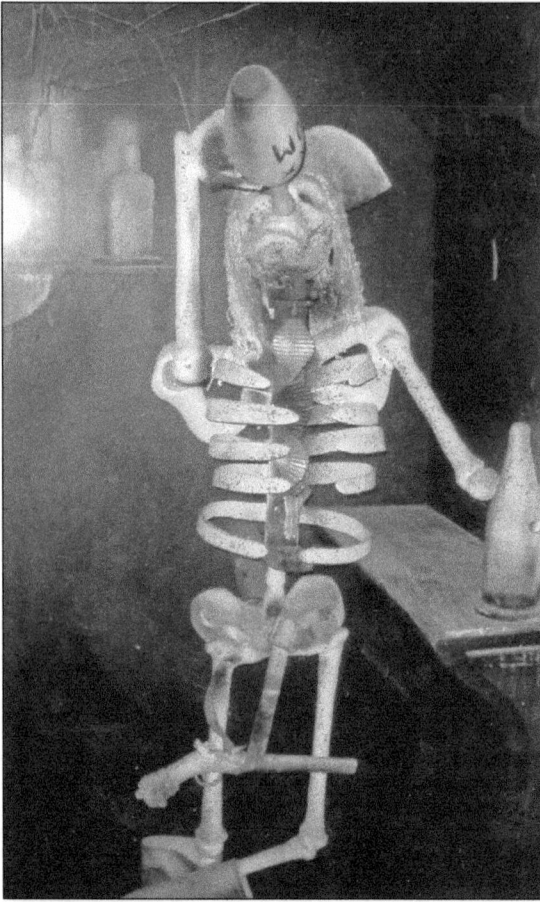

As its name implies, Pirate's Cove has a pirate theme, and the characters inside show pirates in various adventures, including steering the boat, consuming bottles of rum, and fighting off sea creatures. (Both, DH.)

Pirate's Cove was not the only new attraction added in 1972. At the other end of the park, construction was completed on a new train ride. Named the L. Ruth Express in honor of L. Ruth Moeller, the train is a C.P. Huntington model miniature train manufactured by Chance Rides of Wichita, Kansas, the most popular ride of its type in the world. The L. Ruth Express takes riders from a station in the picnic grove to the far northern end of the park near the kiddie land and back. Nelson laid out the track to accommodate two trains in case the park grew to the point that the extra capacity would be needed. A second train was added in 2012. (Both, JF.)

Along with new attractions, Nelson focused much of the 1970s on replacing older rides with newer ones. Among the first was the Aerial Swing. Dating back to the earliest years of Waldameer Park, the ride had seen numerous upgrades over the years with the original wicker gondolas giving way to airplanes in the 1920s and rocket ships in the 1940s. By the 1970s, customers were looking for something a little more exciting, and the Paratrooper replaced the Aerial Swing in 1973. Built by Frank Hrubetz and Company of Salem, Oregon, it was a flashy addition to the changing midway. (Both, WP.)

In 1977, another older attraction was replaced by a flashier new ride. After 32 years of operation, the Flying Scooter was removed, and in its place, the Spider was installed. Manufactured by Eyerly Aircraft Company of Salem, Oregon, the Spider features six arms with two two-person cars at the end that each spin independently. (JF.)

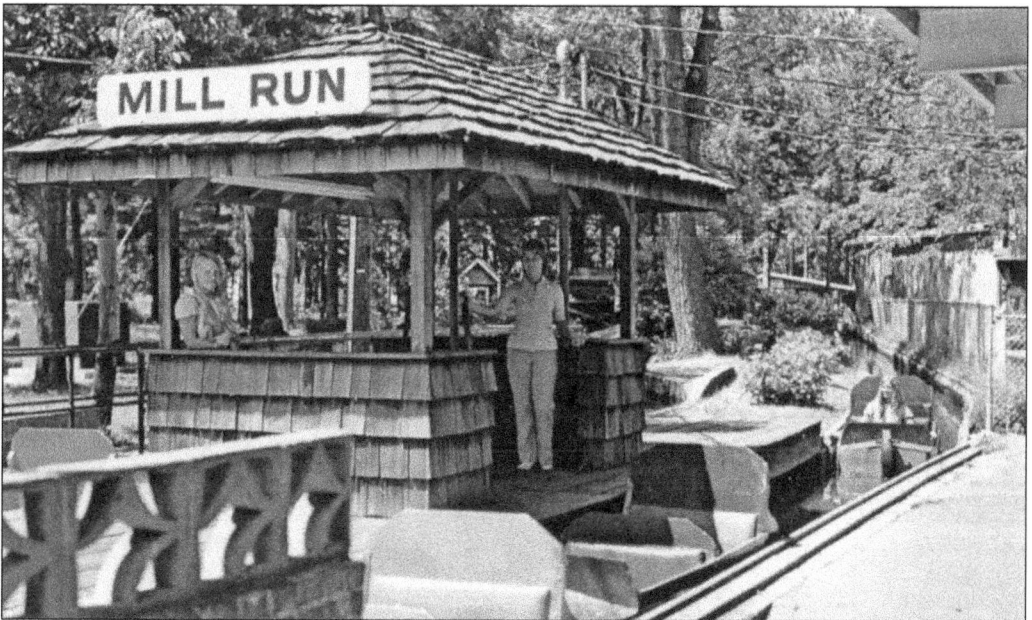

The Mill Run continued to be a popular ride; although, the mild boat ride seemed increasingly out of place at the changing amusement park. It too would eventually be replaced. (JL.)

In 1978, Waldameer Park added the Sky Ride. The ride was built by the O.D. Hopkins Company of Contoocook, New Hampshire, which specialized in producing rides for smaller amusement parks. The Sky Ride's loading station was located at the north end of the park, where Monkey Island had been. It carried riders over the midway to the south end of the park near the recently erected bumper car building where it turned around and returned to the station. (Above, WP; below, RS.)

Four

A SMALL PARK GROWS UP
1980s–1990s

In 1978, after years of hard work, Paul Nelson achieved his dream and assumed complete ownership of Waldameer Park. He succeeded in modernizing the facility but knew that he had his work cut out for him if the park would continue to thrive and grow. At the time, Waldameer was located in one of the most competitive amusement park regions in the country. Larger corporate-owned parks were expanding while smaller facilities were feeling pressure in the face of a decline in the industrial base that provided the company picnics that so many parks depended on.

"I wanted a continuation of the park," said Nelson, wanting to build something that he could pass along to his children. He spoke with his wife, Lane, and came to the conclusion that Waldameer could not survive long term in its current form. It would have to continue growing.

One emerging trend he noticed at the time was the growth of water parks. He saw the addition of one as a logical first step. With the opening of the first phase of Water World in 1986, Waldameer became a pioneer in integrating water attractions with traditional amusement park rides, something now commonplace in the industry. Over the next several years, Nelson worked to build Water World into one of the largest water parks in the state. By the early 1990s, it became time to turn attention back to the amusement park side of the business.

In 1992, a 10-year expansion plan was introduced that would transform Waldameer Park. At the time, Paul Nelson told industry publication *Inside Track* that he "plans to spend enough money on it that it won't go and be turned into a housing development." The rest of the decade was highlighted by constant growth at Waldameer with eight new rides debuting. The park's reputation was increasing, and it was transforming from a local picnic park into a regional destination. As the 20th century came to a close, Waldameer Park's best years were still to come.

Change was in the air for the park in the 1980s. But many old standards remained. Rainbow Gardens remained a popular destination. While the big bands were long gone, the building became a venue for group picnics and special events. (JF.)

At the opposite end of the park, the Merry-Go-Round Grove was also a landmark. Erected for the failed attempt in the 1920s and 1930s to move the carousel and spread out the park, it was pressed into service as a picnic pavilion, a role it continues to play. (JF.)

A quiet day on the midway in 1985 provides no indication of how much the park would change over the next decade and a half. The Paratrooper and Sky Ride are the only attractions visible in this picture. They would soon be joined by many others. (JF.)

Since the 1950s, the kiddie land served as an anchor for the northeast corner of the park. The classic pony cart ride, shown in the foreground in 1985, is still part of today's expanded offerings. (JF.)

In 1984, Waldameer Park replaced its kiddie turnpike ride with the bumper boats. Like bumper cars on water, it provided a cooling ride on a hot summer day. The bumper boats would turn out to be the last major ride added during the 1980s as the park had other plans in mind. (JF.)

Waldameer Park did not leave its smaller customer out in 1984, adding the Lil' Sneak, a kiddie bumper boat ride on the midway. (WP.)

In 1986, the park undertook a project that would transform it forever. Water slides had been around since the mid-1970s but had only just started to be added to traditional amusement parks. Waldameer was a pioneer in adding waterslides to its traditional offerings. Here, construction is well under way in early 1986. (WP.)

Initially, the new water park, dubbed Water World, was a modest operation with just two waterslides and several activity pools. But it was an immediate hit, with visitation increasing dramatically. To accommodate the additional crowds, five additional waterslides were installed in 1989. (WP.)

Included in the 1989 expansion were the free-fall and speed slides, which unlike the more winding slides previously installed, provided a straight drop into a pool at a high rate of speed. (WP.)

Water World opened at just the right time. With water-based attractions sweeping the amusement park industry, it changed the identity of Waldameer Park. Like the early years, when the beach was in operation, it again became the place in Erie to cool off on a hot summer day. (WP.)

In 1990, development of Water World continued with the opening of Bermuda Triangle, a 47-foot tall three slide complex. (WP.)

The $4-million development of Water World culminated with the additions of the Awesome Twosome (left), which opened in 1991, and the Midnight Plunge (right), a trip in complete darkness, which debuted in 1992. (WP.)

By the early 1990s, Water World had grown into one of the largest water parks in Pennsylvania, featuring 11 waterslides, a lazy river, and several activity pools. It had totally transformed Waldameer Park, increasing business dramatically. (JF.)

Development of Water World did not come without sacrifices. In the 1980s, collectors were driving prices for antique carousel animals to record highs. As a result, the park decided to auction its carousel animals and frame following the 1988 season. Over $1 million was raised in the auction, all of which was invested back into expanding Waldameer Park. (Both, JF.)

The carousel had been in operation at Waldameer Park since 1905. In addition to the standard horses, it included a number of other animals such as a lion and a one-of-a-kind elephant that people could sit inside. So while the departure of the ride was sad from a nostalgic perspective, the money invested from the sale did help to guarantee the future of the park. (Both, JF.)

While most of the proceeds for the auction were invested in the continued growth of Water World, a portion was invested in restoring the old carousel building and purchasing a new merry-go-round. Dating back to 1905, the carousel pavilion is the oldest structure in the park. As part of the project, stained-glass windows were installed in the clerestory around the top of the building. (JF.)

The new merry-go-round features 60 horses, all of which jump up and down. Chance Rides of Wichita, Kansas, one of the world's leading manufacturers of merry-go-rounds, manufactured it. (JF.)

A 10-year expansion of the traditional amusement park was announced in 1992. The first new ride added was the Sea Dragon, a swinging ship ride manufactured by Chance Rides. It was installed in a previously undeveloped area next to the Sky Ride. (JF.)

Waldameer had been without a Ferris wheel since the late 1950s, and the park resolved that in 1994 with the addition of the Giant Wheel. Also manufactured by Chance Rides, the 100-foot-tall wheel was placed on a platform built above the bumper boat pond. It stood 180 feet above the surface of Lake Erie, providing a spectacular view of the lake and the nearby Presque Isle peninsula. (JF.)

The addition of the Sea Dragon and Giant Wheel transformed the skyline of Waldameer Park and brought new life to the formerly sleepy northeast corner of the park. (JF.)

Children were not forgotten as the park grew. The Little Toot was added at the base of the Giant Wheel in 1994 as part of the kiddie land. Manufactured by Alter Enterprises of Pompton Plains, New Jersey, the ride is an updated version of the classic handcar ride found in the 1950s at amusement parks throughout the country, including Waldameer. (DH.)

Waldameer Park again returned to Chance Rides in 1995 to add the Wipeout. The high-speed ride has a wobbling motion that resembles a coin as its spinning slows. Wipeout replaced the Flying Coaster. (WP.)

As Waldameer Park started making plans for its 100th anniversary, it became apparent that the Mill Run was due to be replaced. While a nostalgic link to the past, the ride was nearly 70 years old and lacked modern safety features and the thrills the public was looking for. (JF.)

The Mill Run was a sedate ride through the wooded portion of Waldameer Park with a small drop part of the way through. (JF.)

In addition to being dated, the Mill Run occupied a great deal of space with its cement troughs meandering through a grassy area behind the midway. It was space the growing park needed for more productive uses. (JF.)

Once the decision was made to replace the ride, a log flume was the natural choice. To provide the ride, Waldameer turned to O.D. Hopkins, who also built the Sky Ride. At the time, the company was the world's leading manufacturer of water rides. Soon, a large portion of the park was cleared for construction. (JF.)

The $2.5-million ride was named Thunder River and features a 1,300-foot-long trough, a "storm tunnel," and two splashdown hills standing 25 and 40 feet tall. In a link to the past, portions of the waterwheel from the original Mill Run was restored and incorporated into the new attraction. It can be seen in the center of the photograph above. (WP.)

The completed Thunder River was an instant hit and immediately became one of the most popular rides in the park. It was also just the sort of large, high-profile ride needed to demonstrate that the park was on the move. (WP.)

The removal of the Mill Run also provided room for additional attractions. In 1999, Waldameer spent $500,000 to add the Ali Baba. Built by A.R.M. of Wintersville, Ohio, the ride is also known as a flying carpet that sends riders in a towering circular motion, providing thrills and a great view at the same time. (Both, WP.)

Along with the Ali Baba, the park continued to upgrade its kiddie offerings with the addition of two new attractions. In the kiddie land, the Frog Hopper debuted. Built by S&S Worldwide of Logan, Utah, the ride takes children up a 25-foot-tall tower and sends them back to the ground in a bouncing motion. It has become one of the most popular kiddie rides in the industry. (JF.)

Nearby on the main midway, the Big Rigs replaced the Lil' Sneak. Built by Zamperla International of Italy, Big Rigs provides families the opportunity to ride in miniature trucks. Waldameer placed it in a lushly landscaped garden. (DH.)

Despite all the changes at the park, the Comet continued to be its only roller coaster. Its family-oriented design appealed to a wide array of riders, but management knew that the roller coaster lineup would have to grow to serve the larger crowds flocking to the park. (DH.)

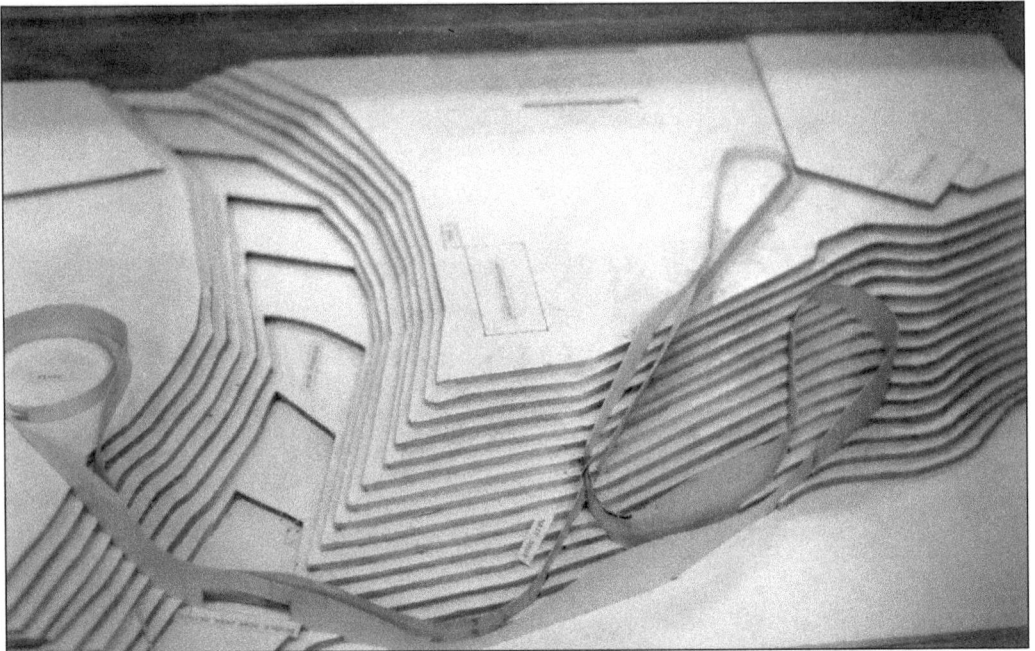

When the 10-year plan was announced in 1992, the intent was to complete it with the construction of a new wooden roller coaster that would re-create, at least in spirit, the original Ravine Flyer. To be called Ravine Flyer II, Waldameer placed a deposit with Custom Coasters, Inc., in 1993, and planning began. By 1996, a model of the proposed ride was being shown. (JF.)

Five

FLYING TO NEW HEIGHTS
2000s–2010s

By the start of the 21st century, most of the family-owned traditional parks that had survived turmoil the previous four decades had learned how to compete, grow, and thrive in the era of the corporate amusement park. Waldameer Park was no different.

As it began its second century, Waldameer Park was in the midst of major transformation. The water park had been completed and was a major draw, and the ride lineup had been updated and expanded. But Paul Nelson, now joined by his daughter Nancy and son-in-law Steve Gorman, was just getting started. It was time to take the park to the next level.

The expansion continued to focus on the traditional amusement park with new rides. In many ways, it can be called the roller coaster decade. Since 1951, the Comet held forth as the only roller coaster in the park. By 2008, it was only one of four, and the new king of the park was the Ravine Flyer II. When it opened in 2008, it represented a culmination of a 15-year quest to bring a signature attraction to the park, and it immediately expanded Waldameer's trade area, drawing people from increasing distances.

Ravine Flyer II opened in the face of another challenging period for the industry. Sky rocketing real estate values combined with excessive debt and ill-advised investments generated a whole new wave of park closings. Included in this round were some of the largest amusement parks ever liquidated, among them, longtime competitor Geauga Lake, outside Cleveland. That further enhanced Waldameer's competitive position and reinforced its long-term future.

In 2012, Paul Nelson announced a new 10-year plan since, as he said, he was "only 79." Additional land has been acquired. Plans call for expanding the water park and again developing the beach area that remains; the park still owns a five-acre parcel. Nelson feels that new land is sufficient to contain his dreams for a few years, but he is always looking ahead. After all, that has defined his relationship with Waldameer Park ever since he arrived in 1945.

Although it has served the same purpose for over 115 years, the main midway at Waldameer Park is a much different place today. As the park has grown, additional amenities have been added, including more games and newly planted trees. (JF.)

The first ride added in the new millennium was a roller coaster. With Ravine Flyer II still making its way through the approval process, the park decided to build a roller coaster its youngest visitors could enjoy. (JF.)

Dubbed the Ravine Flyer III, this ride took the place of the bumper boats in 2000 at the foot of the Giant Wheel. Manufactured by Miler Industries of Portland, Oregon, it is a custom-built family roller coaster constructed over the old bumper boat pond, which added an extra thrill element to the ride. (Both, JF.)

The coaster count continued to grow in 2004 when the Steel Dragon opened at the western end of the park, behind Thunder River and near Rainbow Gardens. The ride represented a new generation of roller coasters that utilizes spinning cars. (Both, WP.)

Built by German ride manufacturer Maurer Sohne, Steel Dragon cost $4 million, stands 50 feet tall, and features nearly 1,400 feet of track. The design of the ride focuses on tight turns and spirals to maximize the spinning of the cars. (Both, DH.)

After spending the first half of the decade tripling the roller coaster lineup, Waldameer Park decided a drop tower should be its next major addition. A relatively new concept in the industry, drop towers haul riders to the top and drop them in a brief free fall before being slowed by magnetic brakes. To gauge guest interest, the park worked with manufacturer A.R.M. of Wintersville, Ohio, to bring in a portable version of the drop tower as a test. From July 5 to July 16, 2006, a 90-foot-tall version of the ride was set up in the northeastern corner of the park, and it was an immediate hit. (Both, WP.)

Based on the results of the test, Waldameer was quick to place an order for one of A.R.M.'s 140-foot-tall models. Soon, a sign was erected next to the Tilt-A-Whirl announcing the addition. (JF.)

Because the park placed the order so early in the season, it was actually ready for operation in November 2006. As a result, Waldameer opened the ride for two days as a charity fundraiser. A naming contest came up with the name X-Scream. By 2007, it was a feature on the park's skyline. (JF.)

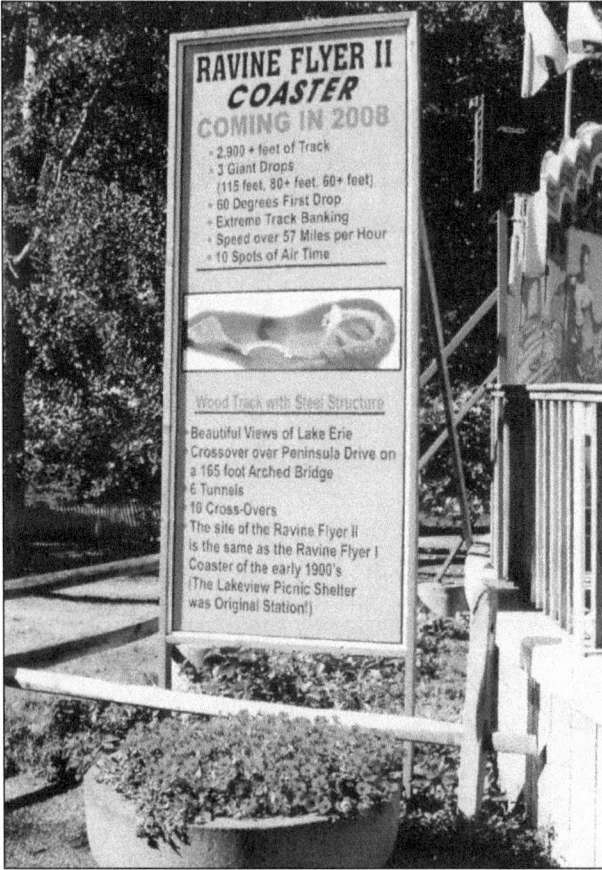

RAVINE FLYER II
COASTER
COMING IN 2008

- 2,900 + feet of Track
- 3 Giant Drops
  (115 feet, 80+ feet, 60+ feet)
- 60 Degrees First Drop
- Extreme Track Banking
- Speed over 57 Miles per Hour
- 10 Spots of Air Time

Wood Track with Steel Structure

- Beautiful Views of Lake Erie
- Crossover over Peninsula Drive on
  a 165 foot Arched Bridge
- 6 Tunnels
- 10 Cross-Overs
- The site of the Ravine Flyer II
  is the same as the Ravine Flyer I
  Coaster of the early 1900's
  (The Lakeview Picnic Shelter
  was Original Station!)

While X-Scream was thrilling riders, Waldameer was able to line up the final series of approvals and construction was ready to begin on Ravine Flyer II. A sign was erected next to the Wipeout in the summer of 2007 announcing its pending arrival. (DH.)

By late-summer 2007, construction was well under way and portions of the structure were already visible to passersby on Peninsula Drive. (WP.)

During the approval process, Custom Coasters had gone out of business, and the park turned to Gravity Group of Cincinnati, Ohio, to design and build the new ride. Construction proceeded rapidly, and by early 2008, the ride's lift hill was signaling passersby that something big was coming to Waldameer Park. (JF.)

In addition to the large drop, the new Ravine Flyer II featured several turns, with some banked up to 90 degrees. (JF.)

One of the most distinctive features of Ravine Flyer II was the fact that it traveled over Peninsula Drive in front of the park. This was a legacy of the original Ravine Flyer, which also crossed the road at almost the same location. After the original Ravine Flyer's demolition, Waldameer Park retained the easement over the road with a mind to the future. (WP.)

The bridge over Peninsula Drive was a construction project in and of itself that connected the two halves of the ride. (WP.)

Once the distinctive arched bridge was completed, it provided a powerful way to promote the park and its new ride to the hundreds of thousands of cars that passed underneath it each summer on the way to Presque Isle State Park. Waldameer Park was required to build a mesh screen around the tracks to keep foreign objects from striking the train or hitting the cars below. They also had to provide extra clearance on the east side of Peninsula Drive in case the state ever needed to widen the road. (Both, WP.)

This aerial view taken in 2011 shows how much the park has grown since the 1980s. The Ravine Flyer II dominates the view starting in the park and crossing Peninsula Drive. Above Ravine

Flyer II are several new attractions from the 1980s and 1990s, including the Sea Dragon, Giant Wheel, and Water World. (WP.)

Once Ravine Flyer II opened on May 17, 2008, the $7.5-million ride had an immediate impact. Dominating the northern end of the midway, its towering lift hill beckoned thrill-seekers. (JF.)

The ride's 80-foot-tall lift hill leads to a 118-foot drop and a turn to the right leading to the bridge over Peninsula Drive at a top speed of 57 miles per hour. (WP.)

Flying through the mesh tunnel, a train travels into the turnaround across the four-lane state highway where it climbs into a second large hill before plunging into the mesh tunnel once again to return to the park. (Above, JF; below, DH.)

After the turnaround and return across Peninsula Drive, the trains fly through a tunnel back into the park where they negotiate a series of steeply banked turns at a high speed. (Both, JF.)

Among the turns the trains pass through on Ravine Flyer II is one banked at 90 degrees. In all, Ravine Flyer II traverses 2,900 feet of track in just a minute and a half. Its construction brought new attention to the park, and new customers who never thought of visiting Waldameer Park flocked to the facility, leading to a record season. The Ravine Flyer II has been ranked the sixth best wood roller coaster by trade publication *Amusement Today*. (Both, JF.)

In 2009, Waldameer Park again expanded the midway to the south. Unlike the failed experiment with the carousel in the 1920s, this time it was a success. An area next to the Merry-Go-Round Grove picnic pavilion was developed into a new $2-million ride area, featuring the Mega Vortex. Manufactured by Zamperla of Italy, the ride has a large spinning disk that seats riders and travels back and forth along a U-shaped track. (Above, JF; left, WP.)

The next expansion occurred in 2011 when an empty area behind the Sea Dragon was developed. While part of the area in the above picture was used for the Ravine Flyer II, there was enough left over to develop the North End. Waldameer purchased three new rides from Zamperla to anchor the area. (Above, DH; below, JF.)

Among the three rides in the North End were the Flying Swings, a 41-foot-tall swing ride; SS Wally, a rocking, spinning tugboat ride; and Wendy's Tea Party, a spinning teacup ride. The L. Ruth Express circled the entire area. (WP.)

While Waldameer Park focused its capital improvements in 2012 on expanding capacity on some of its most popular rides, including the L. Ruth Express, Comet, and Whacky Shack, it also added a new kiddie ride, the Happy Swing. Manufactured by Zamperla, it resembled a large porch swing. Here, crew are putting the finishing touch on the ride prior to its opening. (WP.)

The 2013 season focused on renovating the area between the L. Ruth Express train station and Dodgems. The main attraction was a new Music Express ride, manufactured by Bertazzon of Italy. With 10,000 LED lights, the flashy ride features a high-speed trip around an undulating track. In addition, the Scrambler was moved and renovated with a new color scheme and lighting package. (WP.)

A view from the Sky Ride in 2011 shows a very different Waldameer Park than what existed just two decades earlier. From left to right, the Ravine Flyer II, Sea Dragon, Flying Swings, and Giant Wheel all have been added since the early 1990s. (WP.)

This view from the Giant Wheel shows off Waldameer Park's kiddie land with longtime staples such as the pony carts (top center), boats, and Sky Fighter (center) being joined by the Frog Hopper (left). (JF.)

Looking to the west, a number of new rides dominate the skyline. To the left is Thunder River, the log flume added to celebrate the park's 100th anniversary. Toward the right can be seen the lift hill of Steel Dragon tucked in behind the X-Scream tower. (JF.)

ABOUT THE NATIONAL AMUSEMENT PARK HISTORICAL ASSOCIATION

Since 1984, Jim Futrell has served as historian for the National Amusement Park Historical Association (NAPHA). NAPHA is an international organization dedicated to the preservation and enjoyment of the amusement and theme park industry—past, present, and future.

NAPHA was founded in 1978 by a former employee of Chicago's legendary Riverview Amusement Park (closed 1967) and has grown through the years to include amusement park enthusiasts from around the world.

Membership is open to anyone who enjoys amusement parks. Among the many benefits enjoyed by NAPHA members are *NAPHA News*, a magazine published six times a year; *NAPHA NewsFLASH!!!*, a monthly digital newsletter; conventions at amusement parks; and discounts at select amusement parks.

Throughout its existence, NAPHA has promoted the history of the industry by providing historical information to amusement parks, consultants, and architects, ranging from Time Out Entertainment Centers to Walt Disney Imagineering.

In addition, the International Association of Amusement Parks and Attractions (IAAPA) has often utilized NAPHA as an information resource. Over the years, NAPHA has also been contacted by countless authors, researchers, magazines, newspapers, students, museums, and even advertising agencies and has been credited in everything from books to the *New York Times* to Bruce Springsteen's *Tunnel of Love* record jacket.

The National Amusement Park Historical Association is the world's only organization dedicated to the enjoyment of all aspects of the amusement park. For additional information, visit NAPHA's website at www.napha.org.

Visit us at
arcadiapublishing.com

www.ingramcontent.com/pod-product-compliance
Lightning Source LLC
Chambersburg PA
CBHW050607110426
42813CB00008B/2483